# THE PHILLIP KEVEREN SERIES EASY PIANO

# CELTIC DREAMS

## CONTENTS

— PIANO LEVEL —
EARLY INTERMEDIATE
(HLSPL LEVEL 4-5)

ISBN 978 - 0-634-05716-8

HAL•LEONARD®
CORPORATION
7777 W. BLUEMOUND RD. P.O. BOX 13819 MILWAUKEE, WI 53213

Visit Hal Leonard Online at
**www.halleonard.com**

Visit Phillip at
**www.phillipkeveren.com**

# PREFACE

To my musical friends,

It has been nearly four years since I wrote *The Celtic Collection* (Piano Solo), the first set of arrangements in this series. I have met many of you who have played these arrangements, and your encouragement to write easier versions of these wonderful melodies prompted *Celtic Dreams* (Easy Piano). We have even added a few more tunes for good measure!

My love of these songs remains constant. They always sound fresh to me. They can put me in a great mood or cause me to slow down and reflect. They are simple, yet beautiful.

With best wishes,

*Phillip Keveren*

---

# BIOGRAPHY

Phillip Keveren, a multi-talented keyboard artist and composer, has composed original works in a variety of genres from piano solo to symphonic orchestra. Mr. Keveren gives frequent concerts and workshops for teachers and their students in the United States, Canada, Europe, and Asia. Mr. Keveren holds a B.M. in composition from California State University Northridge and a M.M. in composition from the University of Southern California.

# BENDEMEER'S STREAM

Traditional Irish Folk Melody
Lyric by THOMAS MOORE
Arranged by Phillip Keveren

**Slowly, freely (♩ = 104-112)**

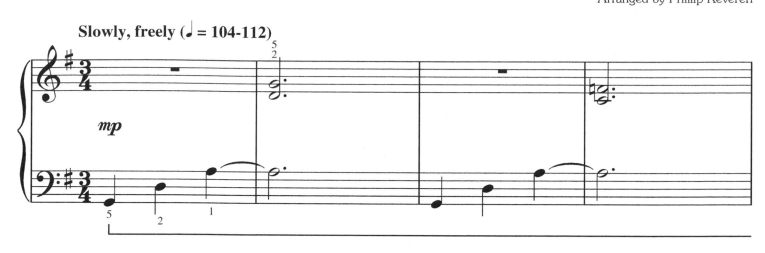

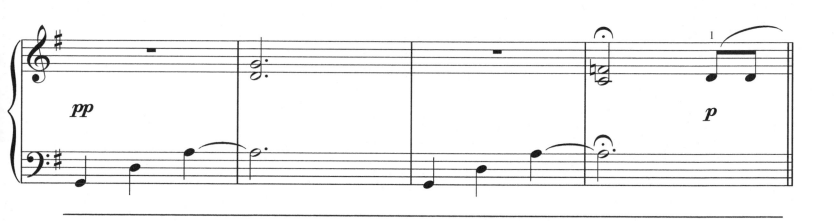

4

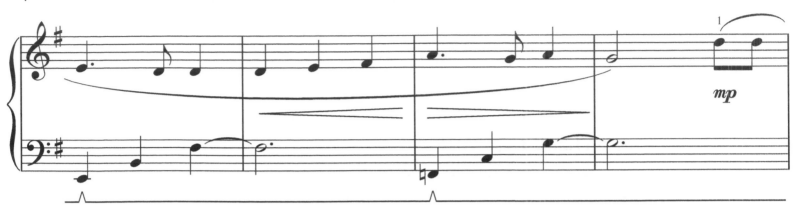

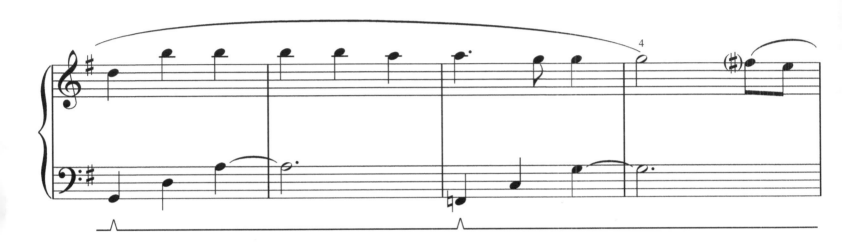

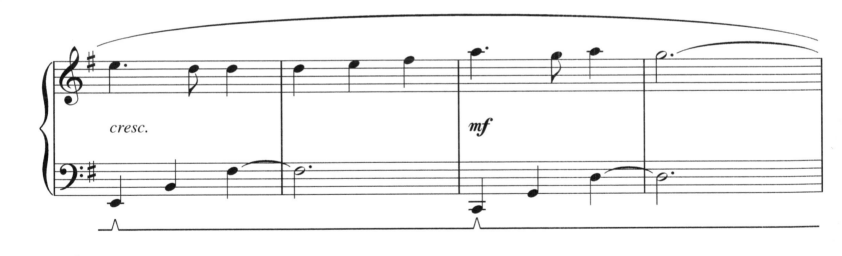

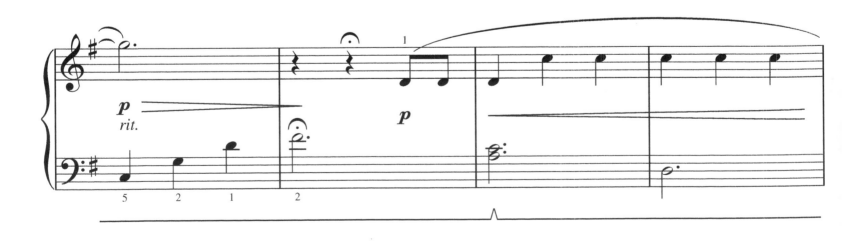

# THE CROPPY BOY

18th Century Irish Folksong
Arranged by Phillip Keveren

Brightly, in 1 (♩. = 66)

# DANNY BOY
## (Londonderry Air)

Lyric by FREDERICK EDWARD WEATHERLY
Music based on the Irish Folksong "Londonderry Air"
Arranged by Phillip Keveren

Slowly, dreamily (♩ = 69)

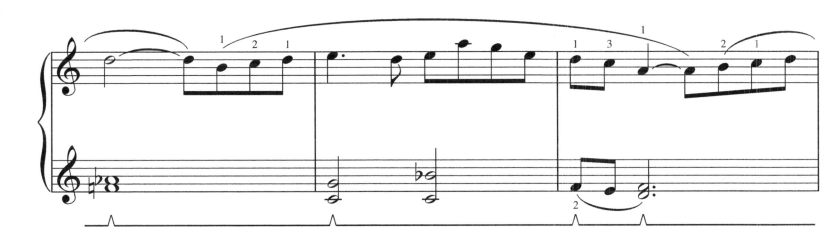

# DOWN BY THE SALLEY GARDENS

Lyric by WILLIAM BUTLER YEATS
Music from the Irish air "The Maids of Mourne Shore"
Arranged by Phillip Keveren

# THE GALWAY PIPER

Irish Folksong
Arranged by Phillip Keveren

**With spirit** (♩ = 118)

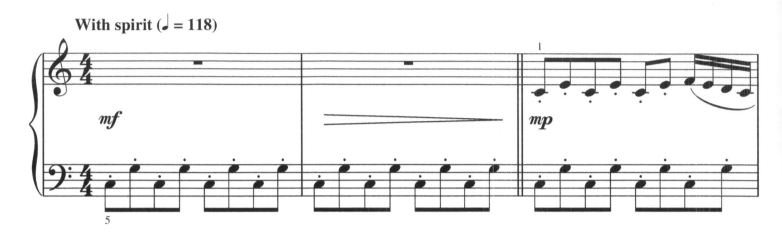

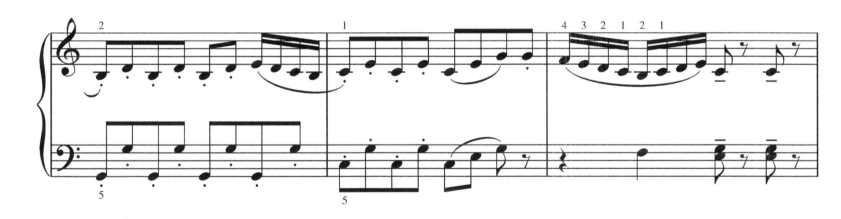

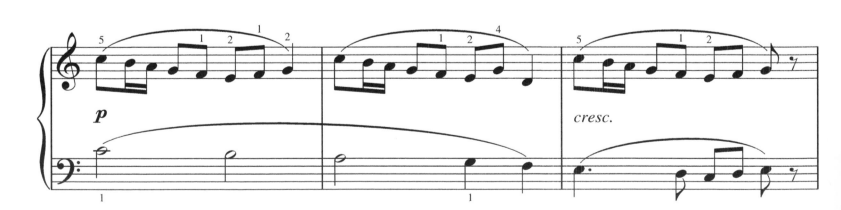

# GARRYOWEN

18th Century Irish Folksong
Arranged by Phillip Keveren

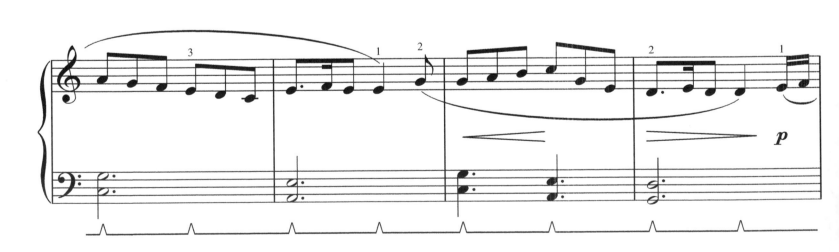

# THE IRISH WASHERWOMAN

Irish Folksong
Arranged by Phillip Keveren

**With driving energy** (♩. = 112)

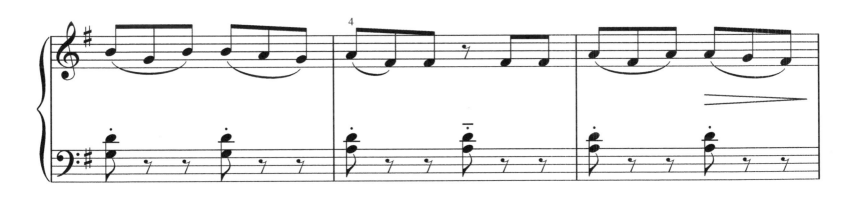

# KITTY OF COLERAINE

Lyric by EDWARD LYSAGHT
Music by AILEEN ROWE
Arranged by Phillip Keveren

Sweetly (♩ = 102)

# THE LARK IN THE CLEAR AIR

Lyric and Music by
SIR SAMUEL FERGUSON
Arranged by Phillip Keveren

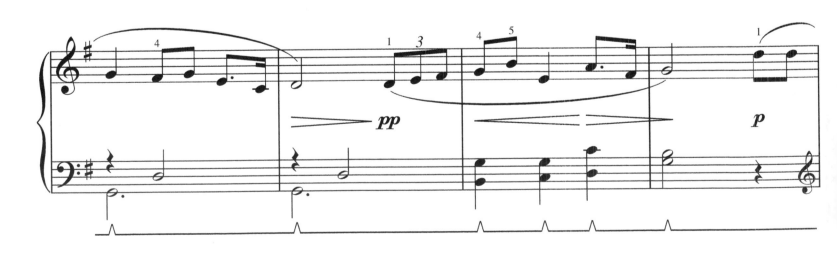

# LET ERIN REMEMBER
# THE DAYS OF OLD

Lyric by THOMAS MOORE
Music based on the Irish Folksong "The Red Fox"
Arranged by Phillip Keveren

# MOLLY BRANNIGAN

Irish Folksong
Arranged by Phillip Keveren

**Moderately slow, with melancholy** (♩ = 69-72)

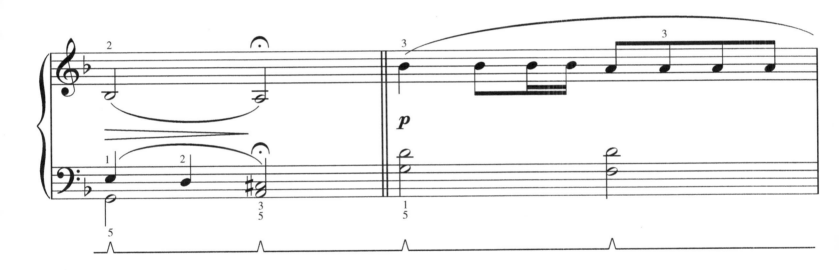

# THE RISING OF THE MOON

Irish Folksong
By JOHN KEEGAN CASEY
Arranged by Phillip Keveren

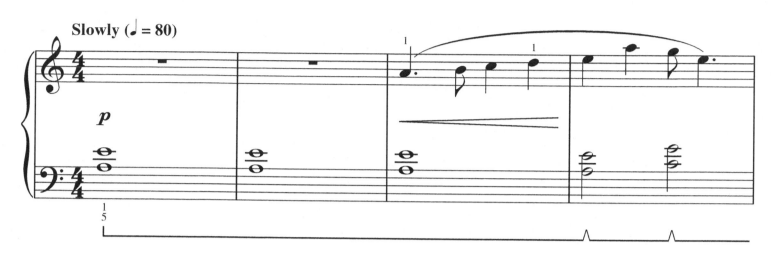

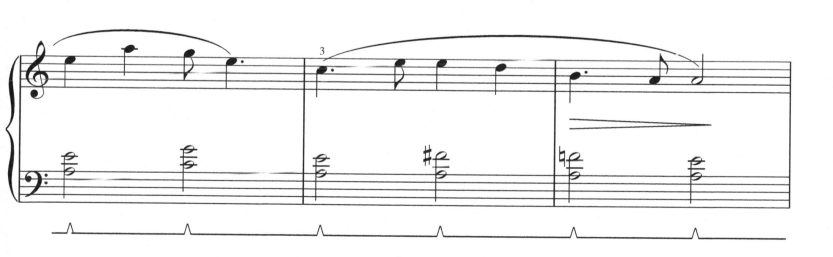

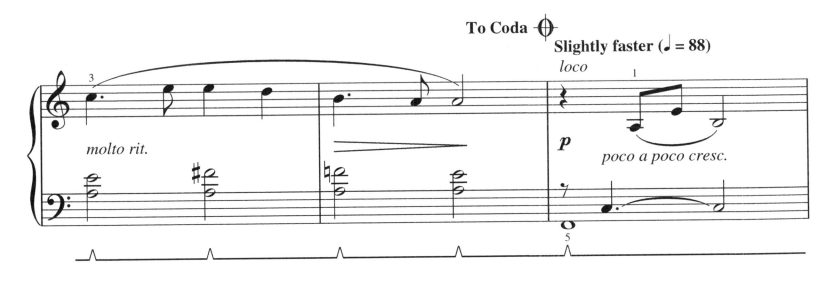

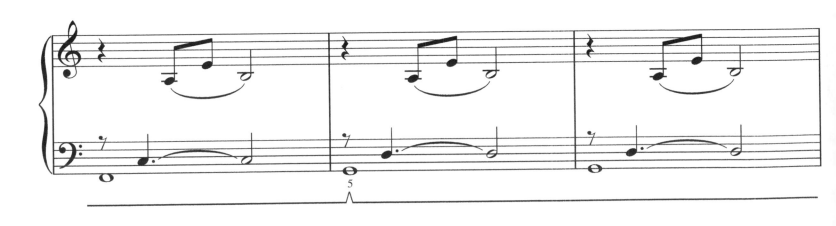

# MOLLY MALONE
## (Cockles & Mussels)

Irish Folksong
Arranged by Phillip Keveren

**Gently flowing** ($\quarternote$ = 112)

# THE PARTING GLASS

Irish Folksong
Arranged by Phillip Keveren

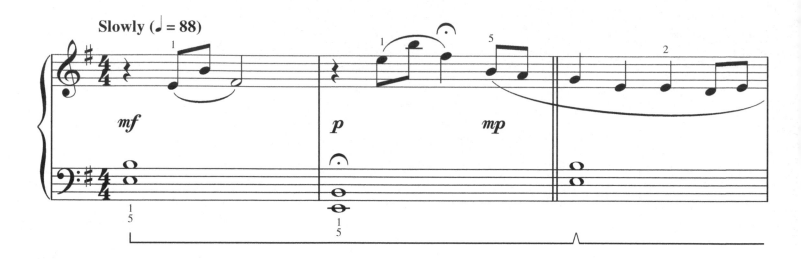

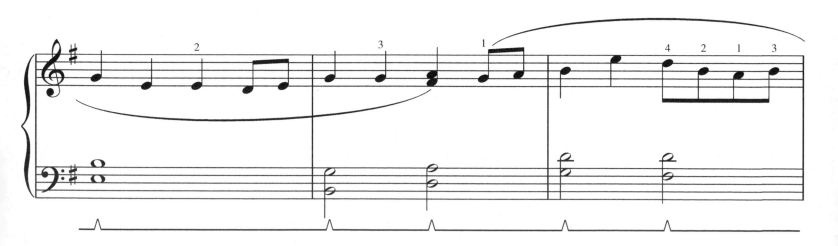

# RORY O'MOORE

Lyric and Music by SAMUEL LOVER
Arranged by Phillip Keveren

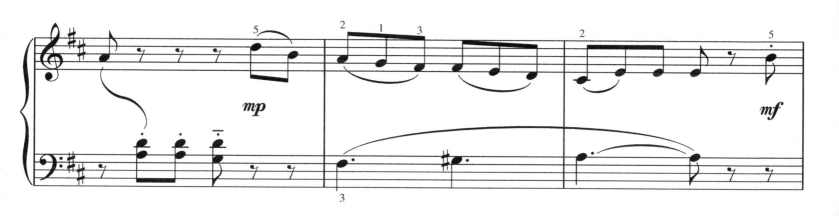

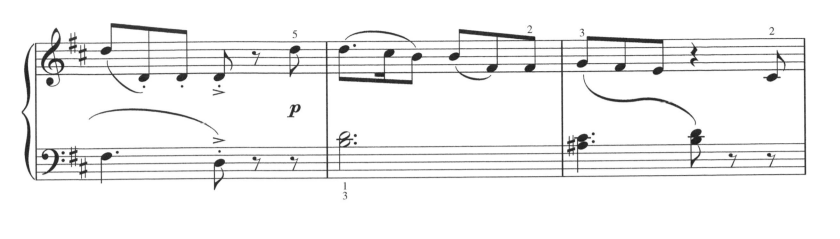

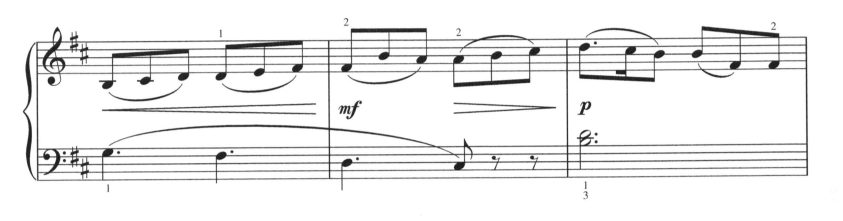

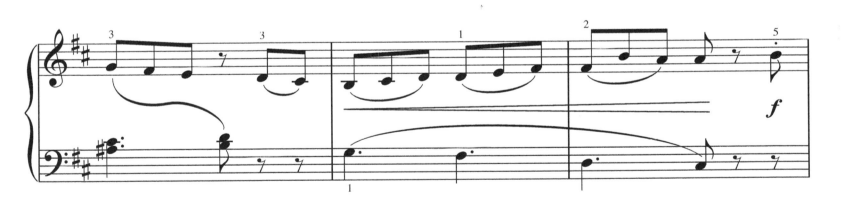

# 'TIS THE LAST ROSE OF SUMMER

Lyric by THOMAS MOORE
Music by RICHARD ALFRED MILLIKEN
Arranged by Phillip Keveren

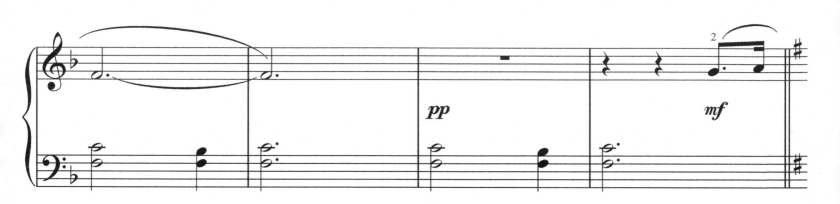

# THE WEARING OF THE GREEN

18th Century Irish Folksong
Arranged by Phillip Keveren

# THE WILD ROVER

Irish Folksong
Arranged by Phillip Keveren

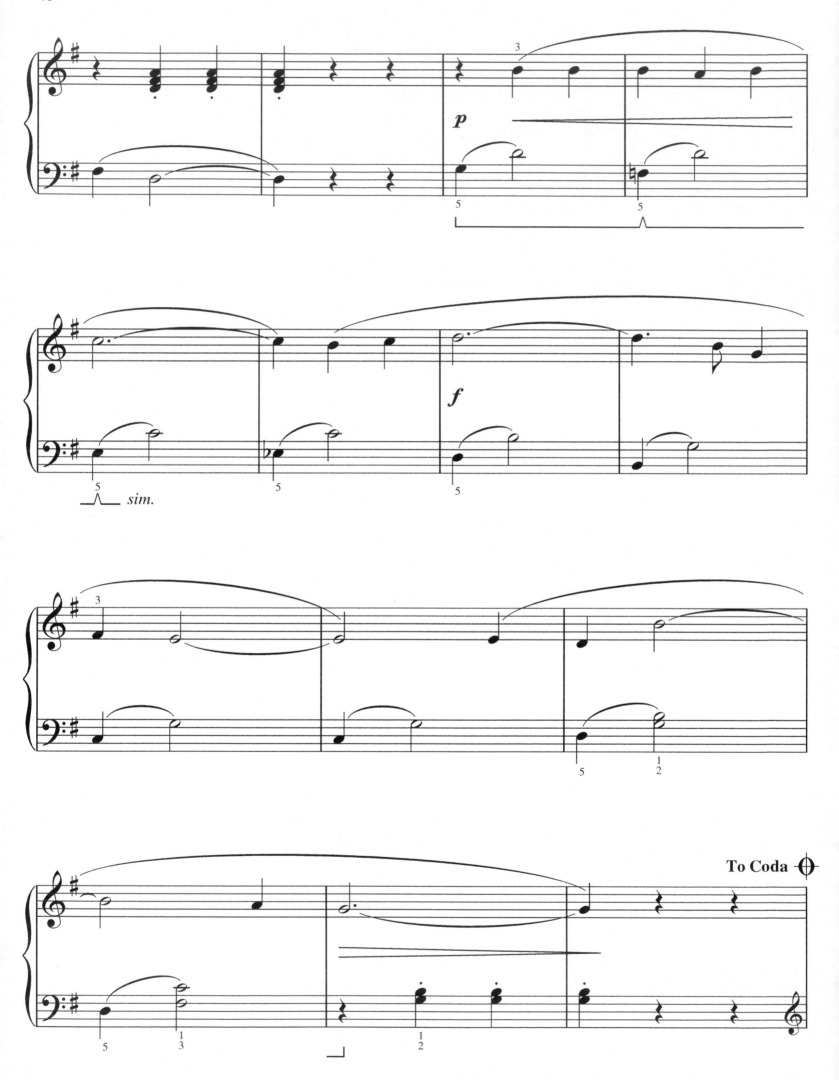

## Bendemeer's Stream
### (Lyric by Thomas Moore)

There's a bower of roses by Bendemeer's stream,
And the nightingale sings 'round it all the day long.
In the time of my childhood 'twas like a sweet dream,
To sit by the roses and hear the bird's song;
That bow'r and its music I ne'er can forget,
But oft when alone in the bloom of the year,
I think, "Is the nightingale singing there yet?
Are the roses still bright by the calm Bendemeer?"

# The Croppy Boy

1. 'Twas early, early in the spring;
   The birds did whistle and sweetly sing,
   Changing their notes from tree to tree,
   And the song they sang was "Old Ireland Free."

2. 'Twas early, early in the night;
   The yeoman cavalry gave me a fright.
   The yeoman cavalry was my downfall,
   And taken was I by the Lord Cornwall.

3. 'Twas in the guardhouse where I was laid,
   And in the parlor where I was tried.
   My sentence passed and my courage low,
   When to Dungannon I was forced to go.

4. As I was passing my father's door,
   My brother William stood at the door.
   My aged father stood there also;
   My tender mother, her hair she tore.

5. As I was going up Wexford Hill,
   Who could blame me to cry my fill?
   I looked behind and I looked before;
   My aged mother I shall see no more.

6. As I was mounted on the scaffold high,
   My aged father was standing by.
   My aged father did me deny,
   And the name he gave me was the Croppy Boy.

7. 'Twas in the Dungannon this young man died,
   And in Dungannon his body lies.
   And you good people that do pass by,
   Oh, shed a tear for the Croppy Boy.

# Danny Boy
## (Londonderry Air)
### (Lyric by Frederick Edward Weatherly)

1.  Oh, Danny Boy, the pipes, the pipes are calling
    From glen to glen and down the mountainside.
    The summer's gone, and all the roses falling;
    It's you, it's you must go and I must bide.
    But come ye back when summer's in the meadow,
    Or when the valley's hush'd and white with snow;
    'Tis I'll be there in sunshine or in shadow.
    Oh, Danny Boy, oh Danny Boy, I love you so!

2.  But if he come, when all the flow'rs are dying,
    And I am dead, as dead I well may be,
    Ye'll come and find the place where I am lying,
    And kneel and say an *Ave* there for me.
    And I shall hear, tho' soft your tread above me,
    And all my dreams will warm and sweeter be.
    If you will not fail to tell me that you love me,
    Then I shall sleep in peace until you come to me!

# Down by the Salley Gardens
### (Lyric by William Butler Yeats)

1. Down by the salley gardens my love and I did meet.
   She passed the salley gardens with little snow-white feet.
   She bid me take love easy, as the leaves grow on the tree.
   But I, being young and foolish, with her did not agree.

2. In a field by the river my love and I did stand,
   And leaning on my shoulder she laid her snow-white hand.
   She bid me take life easy, as the grass grows on the weirs.
   But I was young and foolish, and now am full of tears.

# The Galway Piper

1. Ev'ry person in the nation
   Or of great or humble station
   Holds in highest estimation
   Piping Tim of Galway.
   Loudly he can play, or low;
   He can move you, fast or slow.
   Touch your hearts or stir your toe,
   Piping Tim of Galway.

2. When the wedding bells are ringing,
   His the breath that stirs the singing.
   Then in jigs the folks go swinging.
   What a splendid piper!
   He will blow from eve to morn,
   Counting sleep a thing of scorn.
   Old is he, but not out-worn.
   Know you such a piper?

3. When he walks the highway pealing,
   'Round his head the birds come wheeling.
   Tim has carols worth the stealing,
   Piping Tim of Galway.
   Thrush and linnet, finch and lark
   To each other twitter, "Hark!"
   Soon they sing from light to dark
   Pipings learnt in Galway.

# Garryowen

1. Let Bacchus' sons be not dismayed,
   But join with me each jovial blade.
   Come booze and sing and lend your aid
   To help me with the chorus.

   *Chorus:*
   Instead of spa we'll drink down ale
   And pay the reck'ning on the nail.
   No man for debt shall go to jail
   From Garryowen in glory.

2. We are the boys that take delight
   In smashing the limerick lights when lighting.
   Through all the streets like sporters fighting
   And tearing all before us. *(To chorus:)*

3. We'll break the windows, we'll break the doors,
   The watch knock down by threes and fours.
   Then let the doctors work their cures
   And tinker up our bruises. *(To chorus:)*

4. We'll beat the bailiffs out of fun,
   We'll make the mayors and sheriffs run.
   We are the boys no man dares dun
   If he regards a whole skin. *(To chorus:)*

5. Our hearts so stout have got us fame,
   For soon 'tis known from whence we came.
   Where'er we go they dread the name
   Of Garryowen in glory. *(To chorus:)*

# Kitty of Coleraine

(Lyric by Edward Lysaght)

1. As beautiful Kitty one morning was tripping
   With a pitcher of milk from the fair of Coleraine,
   When she saw me, she stumbled. The pitcher, it tumbled,
   And all the sweet buttermilk watered the plain.
   "Oh, what shall I do now? 'Twas looking at you, now!
   Sure, sure, such a pitcher I'll ne'er meet again.
   'Twas the pride of my dairy. Oh, Barney McCleary,
   You're sent as a plague to the girls of Coleraine!"

2. I sat down beside her and gently did chide her
   That such a misfortune should give her such pain.
   A kiss then I gave her, and before I did leave her
   She vowed for such pleasure she'd break it again.
   'Twas haymaking season, I can't tell the reason,
   Misfortune will never come single, 'tis plain,
   For very soon after poor Kitty's disaster
   There was not a pitcher found whole in Coleraine.

# The Lark in the Clear Air
(Lyric by Sir Samuel Ferguson)

1. Dear thoughts are in my mind,
   And my soul soars enchanted,
   As I hear the sweet lark sing
   In the clear air of the day.
   For a tender, beaming smile
   To my hope has been granted,
   And tomorrow she shall hear
   All my fond heart would say.

2. I shall tell her all my love,
   All my soul's adoration,
   And I think she will hear me,
   And will not say me nay.
   It is this that gives my soul
   All its joyous elation,
   As I hear the sweet lark sing
   In the clear air of the day.

# Let Erin Remember the Days of Old
### (Lyric by Thomas Moore)

1.    Let Erin remember the days of old,
Ere her faithless sons betray'd her;
When Malachi wore the collar of gold,
Which he won from her proud invader;
When her kings with standards of green unfurl'd
Led the Red-Branch Knights to danger;
Ere the emerald gem of the western world
Was set in the crown of a stranger.

2.    On Lough Neagh's bank as the fisherman strays,
When the clear, cold eve's declining,
He sees the round towers of other days
In the wave beneath him shining!
Thus shall memory often, in dreams sublime,
Catch a glimpse of the days that are over;
Thus, sighing, look through the waves of time
For the long faded glories they cover!

# Molly Brannigan

1. Ma'am dear, did ye never hear of pretty Molly Brannigan?
   In throth, then, she's left me, and I'll never be a man again.
   Not a spot on my hide will a summer's sun e'er tan again,
   Since Molly's gone and left me here alone for to die.
   The place where my heart was you'd aisy rowl a turnip in;
   'Tis as large as all Dublin, and from Dublin to the Divil's Glen.
   If she wish'd to take another, sure she might have left mine back again,
   And not have gone and left me here alone for to die.

2. Ma'am dear, I remember when the milking time was past and gone.
   We strolled thro' the meadow, and she swore I was the only one
   That ever she could love, but oh, the base and cruel one.
   For all that she's left me here alone for to die.
   Ma'am dear, I remember when coming home the rain began,
   I wrapt my friezecoat 'round her and ne'er a waistcoat had I on,
   And my shirt was rather fine drawn, but oh, the false and cruel one.
   For all that she's left me here alone for to die.

3. The left side of my carcass is as weak as water gruel, ma'am.
   There's not a pick upon my bones, since Molly's proved so cruel, ma'am.
   Oh, if I had a blunder gun, I'd go and fight a duel, ma'am.
   For sure I'd better shoot myself than live here to die.
   I'm cool an' determined as any salamander, ma'am.
   Won't you come to my wake when I go the long meander, ma'am?
   I'll think myself as valiant as the famous Alexander, ma'am,
   When I hear ye cryin' o'er me, "Arrah! Why did ye die?"

# Molly Malone
## (Cockles & Mussels)

1. In Dublin's fair city, where girls are so pretty,
   I first set my eyes on sweet Molly Malone,
   As she pushed her wheelbarrow thro' streets broad and narrow,
   Crying, "Cockles and mussels, alive, alive, oh!
   Alive, alive, oh! Alive, alive, oh!"
   Crying, "Cockles and mussels, alive, alive, oh!"

2. She was a fishmonger, but sure 'twas no wonder,
   For so were her father and mother before.
   And they each wheeled their barrow thro' streets broad and narrow,
   Crying, "Cockles and mussels, alive, alive, oh!
   Alive, alive, oh! Alive, alive, oh!"
   Crying, "Cockles and mussels, alive, alive, oh!"

3. She died of a fever, and no one could save her,
   And that was the end of sweet Molly Malone.
   But her ghost wheels her barrow thro' streets broad and narrow,
   Crying, "Cockles and mussels, alive, alive, oh!
   Alive, alive, oh! Alive, alive, oh!"
   Crying, "Cockles and mussels, alive, alive, oh!"

# The Parting Glass

1. O, all the money e'er I had,
   I spent it in good company,
   And all the harm I've ever done,
   Alas! It was to none but me.
   And all I've done for want of wit
   To memory now I can't recall.
   So fill to me the parting glass;
   Goodnight and joy be with you all.

2. O, all the comrades e'er I had,
   They're sorry for my going away.
   And all the sweethearts e'er I had,
   They'd wish me one more day to stay.
   But since it falls unto my lot,
   I gently rise and softly call,
   That I should go and you should not.
   Goodnight and joy be with you all.

3. If I had money enough to spend,
   And leisure time to sit awhile,
   There is a fair maid in this town
   That sorely has my heart beguiled.
   Her rosy cheeks and ruby lips,
   I own she has my heart in thrall.
   Then fill to me the parting glass;
   Goodnight and joy be with you all.

# The Rising of the Moon
(Lyric by John Keegan Casey)

1. Oh! Then tell me, Sean O'Farrell, tell me why you hurry so?
   Hush a while, just hush and listen, and his cheeks were all aglow.
   I bear orders from the Captain, get you ready, quick and soon,
   For the pikes must be together at the rising of the moon!

2. Oh! Then tell me, Sean O'Farrell, where the gathering is to be?
   In the old spot by the river, right well known to you and me.
   One word more, for signal token whistle up the marching tune,
   With your pike upon your shoulder by the rising of the moon!

3. Out from many a mudwall cabin eyes were watching through the night.
   Many a manly breast was throbbing for the blessed warning light.
   Murmurs passed along the valley, like the banshee's lonely croon,
   And a thousand blades were flashing at the rising of the moon!

4. There beside the singing river that dark mass of men were seen.
   Far above the shining weapons hung their own immortal green.
   Death to ev'ry foe and traitor, forward strike the marching tune,
   And, hurrah, my boys for freedom, 'tis the rising of the moon.

# Rory O'Moore
## (Lyric by Samuel Lover)

1. Young Rory O'Moore courted Kathaleen Bawn,
   He was bold as a hawk, and she soft as the dawn.
   He wished in his heart pretty Kathleen to please
   And he thought the best way to do that was to tease.
   "Now Rory, be aisy," sweet Kathleen would cry,
   Reproof on her lip but a smile in here eye.
   "With your tricks I don't know in troth what I'm about,
   Faith you've teased till I've put on my cloak inside out."
   "O Jewel," says Rory, "that same is the way
   You've thrated my heart for this many a day.
   And 'tis pleased that I am and why not to be sure?
   For 'tis all for good luck," says bold Rory O'Moore.

2. "Indeed then," says Kathleen, "don't think of the like,
   For I half gave a promise to soothering Mike.
   The ground that I walk on he loves, I'll be bound."
   "Faith," says Rory, "I'd rather love you than the ground."
   "Now Rory, I'll cry if you don't let me go,
   Sure I dream ev'ry night that I'm hating you so!"
   "Oh," says Rory, "that same I'm delighted to hear,
   For dhrames always go by conthrairries my dear.
   O Jewel, keep dreaming that same till you die,
   And bright morning will give dirty night the black lie.
   And 'tis pleased that I am and why not to be sure?
   Since 'tis all for good luck," says bold Rory O'Moore.

3. "Arrah Kathleen, my darling, you've teased me enough,
   And I've thrashed for your sake Dinny Grimes and Jim Duff.
   And I've made myself drinking your health quite a baste,
   So I think after that I may talk to the Priest."
   Then Rory the rogue stole his arm 'round her neck,
   So soft and so white without freckle or speck.
   And he looked in her eyes that were beaming with light,
   And he kissed her sweet lips, don't you think he was right?
   "Now Rory, leave off, sir, you'll hug me no more,
   That's eight times today that you've kissed me before."
   "Then here goes another," say he, "to make sure,
   For there's luck in odd numbers," says Rory O'Moore.

# 'Tis the Last Rose of Summer

(Lyric by Thomas Moore)

1. 'Tis the last rose of summer left blooming alone.
   All her lovely companions are faded and gone.
   No flower of her kindred, no rosebud is nigh
   To reflect back her blushes or give sigh for sigh.

2. I'll leave thee, thou lone one, to pine on a stem.
   Since the lovely are sleeping, go sleep thou with them.
   Thus, kindly I scatter thy leaves o'er the bed
   Where thy mates of the garden lie scentless and dead.

3. So soon may I follow, when friendships decay
   And from love's shining circle the gems drop away.
   When true hearts lie withered and fond ones are flown,
   Oh, who would inhabit this bleak world alone?

# The Wearing of the Green

(Lyric by Dion Boucicault)

1. Oh, Paddy dear, and did you hear the news that's going 'round?
   The shamrock is forbid by law to grow on Irish ground.
   Saint Patrick's Day no more to keep, his color can't be seen,
   For there's a bloody law agin' the wearing of the green.
   I met with Napper Tandy and he took me by the hand,
   And he said, "How's poor old Ireland and how does she stand?"
   "She's the most distressful country that ever you have seen.
   They're hanging men and women there for wearing of the green."

2. Then since the color we must wear is England's cruel red,
   Sure Ireland's sons will ne'er forget the blood that they have shed.
   You may take the shamrock from your hat and cast it on the sod,
   But 'twill take root and flourish still, though under foot it's trod.
   When the law can stop the blades of grass from growing as they grow,
   And when the leaves in summertime their verdure dare not show,
   Then I will change the color that I wear in my corbeen.
   But till that day, please God, I'll stick to wearing of the green!

3. But, if at last our color should be torn from Ireland's heart,
   Her sons, with shame and sorrow, from the dear old soil will part.
   I've heard whispers of a country that lies far beyond the sea,
   Where rich and poor stand equal in the light of freedom's day.
   Oh, Erin, must we leave you, driven by the tyrant's hand?
   Must we ask a mother's welcome from a strange, but happier land?
   Where the cruel cross of England's thraldom never shall be seen,
   And where, thank God, we'll live and die still wearing of the green.

# The Wild Rover

1. I've been a wild rover for many a year,
   And I've spent all my money on whiskey and beer.
   But now I'm returning with gold in great store,
   And I never will play the wild rover no more.

   **Chorus:**
   And it's no, nay, never,
   No, nay, never, no more
   Will I play the wild rover,
   No, never, no more.

2. I went into an alehouse I used to frequent,
   And I told the landlady my money was spent.
   I asked for a bottle; she answered me, "Nay,
   Such a custom as yours I can get any day." *(To chorus:)*

3. Then out of my pocket I took sovereigns bright,
   And the landlady's eyes opened wide with delight.
   She said, "I have whiskies and wines of the best,
   And the words that I said, sure, were only in jest." *(To chorus:)*

4. I'll go back to my parents, confess what I've done,
   And ask them to pardon their prodigal son.
   And if they caress me as ofttimes before,
   Then I never will play the wild rover no more. *(To chorus:)*